Are There Any "*Apostles*" And "*Prophets*" Today?

By

Minister Stephen D. Allen

Are There Any "*Apostles*" And "*Prophets*" Today?

by Minister Stephen D. Allen
Throne Room Ministries International
P.O. Box 441406
Detroit, Michigan 48244-1406

throneroomministries.detroit@gmail.com

Published by
Glory Cloud Publications
Detroit, Michigan

"*Publishing and Promoting the Kingdom of God throughout all the earth!*"

Dedication

This book is dedicated to all of the Apostles, Prophets, Evangelists, Pastors and Teachers on the planet in order to bring unity in the bond of peace to them all, as one!

I also dedicate this book to my wife, Ellen Allen, who patiently allowed me to continue writing and editing this book until completed.

I also dedicate this book to my Pastor, Apostle Donald Coleman, whose ministry I hold in high esteem because of his godly character.

Finally, this book is dedicated to all of the men and women who are answering the call to Ascension Gift Ministries, world-wide! Have respect for one another in spite of your differences because the eyes cannot say to the heart, I have no need of you because without the heart, the eyes will be completely shut forever and the arm cannot say to the hand, I have no need of you because without the hands, the arms are very, very limited in the ability to fully function in their purpose!

Acknowledgments

I want to acknowledge the men and women of Elohim who deeply imparted into my life the spiritual things necessary for me to accomplish my mission in life. This list does not include every person that impacted my life.

Apostle Donald Coleman – New Breakthrough Church International, Detroit (Pastor)

Dr. Darcelle D. White – Learn the Word Ministries - (Teacher) Livonia MI (A "Teacher" Extraordinaire)

Apostle Ellis L. & Pastor Maria Y. Smith – Detroit, (Pastors)

Prophetess Terri Dawson – Terri Dawson Ministries, Phoenix Arizona

Apostle Jefferson Edwards Jr. - Kansas City (Teacher)

Prophet Lee Williams – Redford MI (Apostle)

Pastor Glenn R. Plummer – Ambassadors for Christ Church Detroit, (Pastor)

Pastor Marvin L. Winans – Perfecting Church Detroit, (Pastor)

Pastor Keith Butler – Word of Faith Southfield MI, (Pastor)

The Late Pastor Roosevelt Bradley Jr. - Truelight Missionary Baptist Church, Detroit (Pastor)

*Mrs. Ruby Turner – (My Spiritual Mother / Intercessor and first year counselor from Grambling Louisiana while at Grambling State University where I received Jesus as Lord)

TABLE OF CONTENTS

INTRODUCTION

Well, here is another "Hot Topic"!

Just as the Doctrine of the Baptism in the Holy Spirit is a "Hot Topic", and has caused division in the Body of Christ, so is the subject of the "Apostles" and "Prophets"!

Our adversary, the devil, has strategically divided us on these two issues and we will discuss the reasons why he war against us so hard regarding this subject!

Many leaders and people believe that the Ascension gifts of Apostles and Prophets are no longer on the earth today.

In this we will look at whether they do not exist or if they actually do exist and we will look at biblical proof that is as clear as day!

I will give you a tip, they actually do exist today and the controversy is caused by the devil himself and we will prove from the bible why he has caused this division!

Let's get started proving this truth!

1
WHAT IS THE "CHURCH"?

Now why would I start this book with this chapter? The answer is very simple, the "Church" is in existence because the very first Apostle, Jesus Christ, started it!

We will discuss the Apostolic Assignment of Jesus in a later chapter, however, discussing the Church, we must discuss Jesus Christ.

All of you leaders and bible scholars, do not skip over this chapter, because you will miss some truths that you may not be aware of.

The word "Church" is the Greek word, "*Ekklesia*" which simply means, "*called out*" ones, speaking of people! Knowing that definition, let's see how the Church actually began.

When Jesus began His ministry, He had already become popular because of His baptism by John the Baptizer and He also caused an uproar with the religious leaders. As He was walking by the sea of Galilee, <u>Andrew</u>, Simon, also named <u>Peter</u>, <u>James</u> and <u>John</u>, the sons of Zebedee, was <u>called out</u> from their jobs as fishermen.

Later, He came across <u>Levi</u>, a tax collector, and called Him and then there is the account of <u>Philip</u> and <u>Nathaniel</u> being <u>called out</u> by Jesus. (See Matthew 4:18-22, Mark 1:16-20, Luke 5:1-11, 28-29, John 1:35-50)

These seven are named in the bible as being called out. Luke 6:12-16 details what happened when He <u>chose</u> the 12 Apostles, It reads, "*Now it came to pass in those days that He went out to the mountains to pray, and continued all night in prayer to God. And when it was day, He <u>called</u> His disciples to Himself; and from them He <u>chose</u> twelve whom He also named <u>Apostles</u>; Simon, whom He also named Peter, and Andrew his brother; James and John; Philip and Bartholomew; Matthew and Thomas; James the son of Alphaeus, and Simon called Zealot; Judas, the son of James, and Judas Iscariot who also became a traitor*". (NKJV)

So, the original twelve Apostles were <u>called</u> and <u>chosen</u> by Jesus, Himself. (Keep this is mind)

Having chosen His twelve Apostles, He continued gathering disciples to Himself as people chose to believe in Him and then followed Him.

These Apostles became the ones that Jesus directly poured into on a very personal level. Jesus was *downloading* His assignment into them and also *demonstrating* what His assignment requires which is, <u>preaching</u>, <u>teaching</u>, <u>healing</u>, <u>casting out devils</u>, and <u>confronting the religious establishments</u> under the old covenant of the Law of Moses.

This was the beginning of the gathering of the "Church", the ekklesia, the called out ones. The assignment for the Church today still has not changed, it is the same assignment that Jesus taught and demonstrated to the Apostles and the disciples while He was conducting His earthly ministry.

The "Church" today need to get back to doing the work that Jesus did and please the Father! We are in dire need of "Order in the Church"!

2
"ORDER IN THE CHURCH!"

In the court room, when things are beginning to get chaotic and people are speaking very angrily and out of turn, interrupting the attorneys or the judge, the judge will strike his gavel and say, "order in the court"! Our Judge has struck His gavel in Heaven and has declared, "Order in the Church"!

Exactly what is "order"? I will give you the definitions that pertain to the "order" in the Church. **1** the arrangement of people or things according to a particular sequence or method. **2** a state in which everything is in its right place. **3** an instruction that must be obeyed; a command. **4** the set procedure followed in a meeting, court of law, or religious service.

Using these definitions, we will look at what is not in "order" in the Church. First of all, when Jesus ascended on high, He gave "gifts" unto men, Ephesian 4:7-8, 11-12 details this transaction as: *"But to each one of us grace has been given as Christ apportioned it. This is why it says: 'When he ascended on high, he led captives in his train and gave __gifts__ to men.' 'It was he who gave some to be apostles, some to be prophets, some to be evangelists, and some to be pastors and teachers, to prepare God's people for works of service, so that the body of Christ may be built up until we all reach unity in the faith and in the knowledge of the Son of God and become mature attaining to the whole measure of the fullness of Christ"*. (NIV)

Here we have "an arrangement of people" according to the definition of "order"; we have the apostle, the prophet, the evangelists, and the pastors and teachers. This order will not change until the gift-giver changes it or refuses to give them anymore. There is nothing in scripture that indicates that this order has changed in any way.

So the first thing to be put back in order is the fact that all of these "gifts" given by Jesus are still the order that He has established and has not called any of them back; His gifts are without repentance and He does not want them back!

There are many people calling themselves "Apostles" and "Prophets" and do not have the equipping to fulfill that calling. Apostles are sent with a specific mission and an anointing to accomplish that mission and it is known by that Apostle and their lives are focused on that assignment.

A Great Apostle said that some of these ministers need to be called into the court of heaven and reprimanded for declaring themselves to be something that they are not and functioning with that title without being licensed or given that **gift**.

Another thing that is <u>out of order</u> is the fact that there are ministers who believe that they are doing God a service by "calling out" other ministers and labeling them as "false teachers"! This action, being done incorrectly, is a tool of the adversary to cause division and strife in the body of Christ.

I want to publicly say that Kenneth Hagin, Kenneth Copeland, Fred Price, Creflo Dollar and some others are not "false" teachers! A "false" teacher is a "teacher" that is <u>deceitful</u> and wicked, a spurious (fake or phony) teacher who propagates (promotes an idea or knowledge) erroneous (wrong or incorrect) Christian doctrines! (Strong's Concordance)

Let's see what the bible says concerning "false" teachers. 2 Peter 2:1-3 says, *"But there were false prophets among the people, just as there will be false teachers among you. They will secretly introduce destructive heresies* (belief or opinion that goes against traditional religious doctrine), *even denying the sovereign Lord who bought them – bringing swift destruction on themselves. Many will follow their shameful ways and will bring the way of truth into disrepute* (the state of having a bad reputation). *In their greed, these teachers will exploit you with stories they have made up. Their condemnation have long been hanging over them, and their destruction has not been sleeping."* (NIV) emphasis added

These "false" teachers know that they are being divisive based upon their own motives. They do not worship Jesus Christ and lead people away from the full truth and even saying that He is not the true Messiah and denying our redemption through His blood.

We know of many teachers who are doing this and that they deny that Christ is the Son of God or that there is another kind of Jesus for us as a people! These are damnable heresies from "false" teachers.

We must use wisdom when trying to declare anyone being false, you can tell the root system of a person by looking at the fruit of that persons life!

It is easy to teach a doctrine that is in error of scripture or an interpretation that is based upon human reasoning rather than scriptural truths. This does not make one a "false" teacher, it simply means that they need to do more studying or get with others to correctly divide the word if they need help. We all should be open to corrective criticism when it deals with biblical doctrines.

All I am saying about the false teacher proclamations is to be aware of the fact that our adversary, the devil, always wants to sow discord among the brethren and cause division and strife and confusion so that he can skip away and continue to destroy the lives of people who desperately need true ministers to truly minister to them!

Now regarding "false" Prophets, there are none in the Body of Christ, only those who "falsely" prophesy and this is another thing that is <u>out of order</u> in the Church because there are many among us! We must only say what the Lord has us to say or keep our mouths shut!

Everyone that prophesies is not a Prophet, however, every Prophet will prophesy and those with the manifestation of the gift of prophecy will prophesy. A false prophet is one who is not of God, but of the devil!

Jesus Himself said, *"Watch out for false prophets. They come to you in sheep's clothing, but inwardly they are ferocious wolves. By their fruit you will recognize them. Do people pick grapes from thorn bushes, or figs from thistles? Likewise every good tree bears good fruit, but a bad tree bears bad fruit."* (Matthew 7:15-17) NIV

The Apostle John said, *"Dear friends, do not believe every spirit* (human, angel, demon)*, but test the spirits to see whether they are from God, because many false prophets have gone out into the world. This is how you recognize the Spirit of God: every spirit that acknowledges that Jesus Christ has come in the flesh is of God, but every spirit that does not acknowledge Jesus is not from God. This is the spirit of the antichrist, which you have heard is coming and even now is already in the world".* (1 John 4:1-3) emphasis added

We know of many false prophets that are in the world today. Look at every religion that has a man or an object set aside and said to be the one sent from God to help us but they are not Jesus Christ, they are all false prophets.

I will name a few, The Mormons, The Jehovah's Witnesses, Islam and others. They deny that Jesus Christ is the Son of God and they also deny that He is the third part of the God-head, which is known as the Trinity, thereby declaring themselves as antichrist and their founders as "false prophets"!

The truth will still make people free when they recognize that Jesus is the Way, the Truth and the Life and that no one comes to the Father but by Him and only Him! (John 14:6)

There is one more thing that is <u>out of order</u> in the Church that I would like to bring up; the ministry of the Evangelist. First of all, will all of those who have a legitimate call to be an Evangelist please stand up and be noticed and appreciated! I'm referring to the "gift" that was given by Jesus.

There are only three times that the Evangelist is mentioned in the Bible. Acts 21:8 refers to Philip the Evangelist, 2 Timothy 4:5 refers to those who are preaching to *"do the work of an Evangelist, fulfill your ministry.* Ephesians 4:11 is the place where it is recorded that Jesus Christ gave that gift to some people.

The Strong's definition for the word Evangelist is, *"a preacher of the gospel, to announce the good news"*. There are many people who are calling themselves "Evangelist" who do not have any signs in their ministry that an Evangelist usually demonstrate. First of all, Evangelist win people to Christ more often than others because they have a "gift" to dispense the good news in convincing ways that people can see and understand.

Evangelist Billy Graham is a good example of what I am talking about. The only thing about him is that he did not have any miraculous works accompanying the messages that he preached, however, people responded.

I do not believe that Billy Graham had the mighty Baptism in the Holy Spirit which is the empowering force of the Holy Spirit, enabling people to do the works of Jesus, such as, healing the sick.

11

Let's look at Philip the Evangelist. Philip was chosen as one of the seven men of good reputation, full of the Holy Spirit and wisdom to minister as Deacons to serve the people. (Acts 6:1-7)

In Acts 9:26-40, we see Philip operating in his Evangelist gift as he is sent to a specific location to meet with a very important Ethiopian man. This man was an Ethiopian Eunuch of great authority under Candace, the queen of the Ethiopians. He had charge of all her treasury, and had come to Jerusalem to worship.

Just a note here, the Ethiopians had in their lineage a child from Solomon and the Queen of Sheba when they came together, and he was a grandson of King David and an heir to the throne of Israel. (2 Chronicles 9:1-12) The Jewish Ethiopians were worshiping the Lord as the Jews did in Israel and a trip to Israel to worship was a very special event!

He was on his way home and was sitting in his chariot and reading the book of the Prophet Isaiah when the Spirit of the Lord said to Philip to go over to his chariot and stay near it.

Philip ran up to the chariot and heard him reading Isaiah and asked if he understood what he was reading and the Ethiopian asked how could he unless someone guides him.

He invited Philip into his chariot to explain who a scripture was referring to, the scripture reads as so, "*He was led as a sheep to the slaughter; and as a lamb before its shearer is silent, so He opened not His mouth. In His humiliation His justice was taken away. And who will declare His generation? For His life is taken from the earth*". (Acts 8:32-33) NKJV

The bible says, "*Then Philip opened his mouth, and beginning at this scripture, preached Jesus to him.*" As they went down the road, the Ethiopian asked "*what hinders me from being baptized*" and Philip answered, "*If you believe with all your heart, you may*" and he answered, "*I believe that Jesus Christ is the Son of God*"!

The two of them went into the water and he was baptized and when they came out of the water, "*the Spirit of the Lord caught Philip away, so that the eunuch saw him no more; and he went on his way rejoicing*".

So this Evangelist preached Jesus to the Ethiopian eunuch and the Ethiopian then took the good news of his experience and knowledge back to Ethiopia and that nation became impacted with the gospel as a result!

That is what a New Covenant Evangelist of Christ does in their ministry and we are not seeing that on a large scale today! We barely hear about an Evangelist unless it's Reinhard Bonnke or Benny Hinn who have miracles, signs, and wonders accompanying their ministries!

We desperately need a move of the Spirit of God among those called and anointed to be an Evangelist to effectively preach the gospel of Christ to this generation. Outside of the local church is where they are needed!

There are many other things that are <u>out of order</u> in the Church and we need the Apostles and Prophets to address these issues globally. We need to step-up-our-game and be about our Father's business. The false religious systems need to be effectively addressed in the world today, but we need "<u>ORDER IN THE CHURCH</u>" right now!

3
WHAT IS THE STRATEGY OF THE DEVIL?

In this chapter we are going to expose the strategic maneuvers that Satan has been using against us in a very effective way. The kingdom of darkness has a very effective communication system and their goal is to "divide and conquer"!

Let's look at their hierarchy and how they operate. Ephesians 6:10-12 says, *"Finally, my brethren, be strong in the Lord and in the power of His might. Put on the whole armor of God, that you may be able to stand against the wiles of the devil. For we do not wrestle against flesh and blood, but against <u>principalities</u>, against <u>powers</u>, against the <u>rulers of the darkness of this age</u>, against <u>spiritual hosts of wickedness</u> in the heavenly places."* (NKJV)

This hierarchy displays the details of their system and they all communicate with one another and team up against those coming against them with the Truth! They are all fallen angels, however, they have various evil functions.

The principalities are the princes, chiefs, rulers, magistrates of various Nations, Cities, People or Race where Satan has established his power and authority.

The Prophet Daniel had an encounter with Gabriel, the arch-angel of God who told him what would become of the nation of Israel but it took him twenty-one days to get the answer to Daniel. Gabriel said that the first day that he prayed, he was heard *"But the prince of the Persian kingdom resisted me twenty-one days"*. (Daniel 10:12-13) NIV

The powers are "authorities", or delegated influences of control, such as, terrorism, drug cartels, and the such. I believe that they carry out orders given out by the Principalities over their area which are accountable to Satan, himself.

The rulers of the darkness of this age are "world-rulers" who probably dominate societies with various evils, such as false religions and idolatry.

16

The <u>spiritual hosts of wickedness in heavenly</u> <u>places</u> is "depravity which is *(making someone immoral or wicked)*, causing malice (the desire to harm someone), plots (secret plans to do something illegal or wrong), sins, and iniquity (against God).

They are closer to the function of "demons", which are "disembodied spirits" but they probably do not seek to possess the bodies of people yet wield controlling powers and influences over them.

The Apostle Paul does not go into details regarding their specific functions, however, we know that they are all against God and His Word and they seek to destroy all of mankind by causing constant rebellion against God.

Let's look at the meaning of the word "strategy". Strategy is a plan designed to achieve a particular long-term aim, it also means the art of planning and directing military activity in a war or battle; often contrasted with tactics which is (the art of directing and organizing the movement of armed forces and equipment during a war).

This is exactly what Satan has been orchestrating to make war against the Kingdom of God, Whose Name is Elohim! Satan has an evil agenda that he does not want us to realize. Let's look at some of them.

The first thing that we know is the he wants to be worshiped! He wants to cause mankind to rebel against what God has established in the earth, and he wants to control mankind and keep the races divided from each other with racism and bigotry.

His first attack was against Adam and Eve as he deceived Eve and caused Adam to commit treason in following her in the defiance of God.

His second attack was against their sons dividing them against one another and ultimately influencing Cain to murder Abel when God rejected his worship and accepted Abel's worship.

The attack then ensued against all of their descendants causing them to be so wicked and evil that it repented God that He made man and flooded the earth, saving only Noah and his family.

Satan then attacked Ham, causing him to sin against his father, Noah. Noah then cursed Ham's son, Canaan, and this led to battles against family for promised territory as a result of the curse.

Satan then attacked the nation of Israel where God chose to place His name and his focus remained on them until Christ entered the earth, then his focus was on Jesus, the Savior of the world!

Before Jesus came into the earth, Satan heard many prophecies about the Messiah who was to come to Israel. He also remembered what God said to him in the garden regarding the "Seed" of Eve that would crush his head. Satan did not know what to expect!

Satan did everything in his power to destroy Jesus as a child and then he tried to deceive Him when he told Him to worship him and that he would give Him the kingdoms of the world.

Satan knew that if Jesus had worshiped him, that he would have achieved a great victory because he knew that Jesus was God–the Son, who had him kicked out of heaven! He also knew that that would displease the Father. It was the same kind of attack that he made on the first Adam and his wife, named Eve.

His strategies never change because he is still seeking the same goal of worship, control and defiance against God!!

Now I want to discuss Satan's attack against the Church, the world-wide Body of Jesus Christ!

Before I go to his strategies, I want to clarify the basic mission of the Church. We are called out from the world to continue the ministry of Jesus Christ in the earth to let everyone know what He has done for all of us until He returns!

As I said, the strategy of Satan does not change because he has the same goals from when He was kicked out of heaven and then, in creation, when he saw God creating the first man, Adam.

The attack from Satan is against "WHAT HAS GOD SAID"! Jesus is the Living Word of God and everything that He taught, Satan is fighting against, including <u>bringing the world into unity in Christ</u>!

According to Mark 6:5-6, the Apostle Mark recorded that Jesus could do no miracles in His hometown except lay his hands on a few sick people and heal them because of their lack of faith.

If we do not radically believe and proclaim what Jesus has said, we will ultimately fail in our mission to make disciples of all nations!

Can you believe that Jesus, Himself was limited in His ability to perform and minister because of their own lack of faith in Him?

There are so many things that limit our ability to effectively minister to mankind and the Apostles and Prophets of today are called to confront those things!

Well, that is the truth and Satan knows that so he fights against us in many ways, doctrinal belief, worship, love, unity, oneness in Christ among the nations of the world and whether or not if Apostles and Prophets really do exist today!

You need to understand that the first thing Satan noticed about the disciples was that after Jesus had chosen His twelve, He called them Apostles! He had already known about the Prophets and their function from the time of Abraham, so he did not know what to expect from the Apostles!

In our next chapter we will see why Satan fights against the truth that Apostles and Prophets do exist today! Many leaders do not believe this to be true, which is a travesty (a misrepresentation of the Truth) because the Apostles and the Prophets are the first two ministries established in the earth!

4
WHAT IS THE FOUNDATION OF
THE CHURCH?

What exactly is a "foundation" because there are a few different definitions but we will see which ones apply to the Church and then see how they apply.

We will look at four different definitions for foundation. **1.** "a basis on which something is grounded (*a relation that provides the foundation for something*). **2.** The lowest support of a structure. **3.** The education or instruction in the fundamentals (*serving as an essential component, far-reaching and thoroughgoing in effect especially on the nature of something, any factor that could be considered important to the understanding of a particular business*) of a field of knowledge.

4. The fundamental assumptions from which something is begun or developed or calculated or explained". Let's look closer at these definitions.

1. A foundation is "<u>a basis on which something is grounded</u>, (a relation that provides the foundation for something)

In Matthew 7:24-27, Jesus spoke about the man who <u>built his house on the rock</u> and the man that did not build his house on the rock. He said when the rain came down and the streams rose, and the winds blew on that house that it <u>did not fall</u> because it had its **foundation on the rock**.

Deuteronomy 32:3-4 says, "*I will proclaim the name of the Lord. Oh, praise the greatness of our God! He is **the Rock,** His works are perfect, and all His ways are just.*" (NIV)

The Church, the world-wide Body of Jesus Christ is grounded on and in <u>the Rock</u>! **2.** A foundation is "<u>the lowest support of a structure</u>". The lowest support of anything must always be the strongest part and able to bear the weight of the entire structure.

Romans 9:33 says, "*See, I lay in Zion a stone that causes men to stumble and a rock that makes them fall, and the one who trusts in him will never be put to shame.*"

Jesus is that Stone and that Rock that we all rely upon and on whom we base our existence as the Church, the people of God.

3. A foundation is "the education or instruction in the fundamentals of a field of knowledge, (serving as an essential component, far-reaching and thoroughgoing in effect especially on the nature of something, any factor that could be considered important to the understanding of a particular business)".

Jesus provided the "education" and "instruction" regarding God and His Kingdom and what we all needed in order to be reconciled back unto God and to live a holy life.

The Apostles and Prophets, Evangelists, Pastors and Teachers went about giving the same education and providing the same instructions that Jesus gave to them.

4. A foundation is "<u>the fundamental assumptions from which something is begun or developed or calculated or explained</u>".

We know that the Church began when Jesus breathed upon the disciples before He ascended and they were immediately born again. (John 20:22) Jesus birthed the Church into the earth; He is our starting point from which we all extend from without any assumptions, but only the absolute Truth!

John 15:5 says, *"I am the vine; you are the branches. If a man remains in Me and I in him, he will bear much fruit; apart from Me you can do nothing".* (NIV)

Ephesians 2:19-20 says, *"You are no longer foreigners and aliens, but fellow citizens with God's people and members of God's household, built on the <u>foundation of the apostles and prophets,</u> with <u>Jesus</u> <u>Christ</u> Himself as <u>the</u> <u>chief</u> <u>cornerstone</u>".* (NIV)

2 Peter 3:2 says, *"I want you to recall the words spoken in the past by the holy prophets and the command given by our Lord and Savior through your apostles."*

This clearly shows that the Apostle and Prophets are the foundation of the house of God, the Church that has been built upon the Rock, a solid foundation, that is, the Christ.

I want to say that the original twelve Apostles of the New Covenant and the Prophets of the Old Covenant are the solid foundation that the Church is built upon. The things that they were commanded to say is the actual foundation!

The Church is the continuation of the ministry that Jesus began, and the present day Apostles and Prophets are also the continuation of that ministry in the earth!

5
WHY DOES THIS ERRONEOUS TEACHING EXISTS TODAY?

Satan knows exactly what he is doing and knows exactly what is going on because he constructed it; he is the author (*someone who originates or causes or initiates something*) of confusion!!!

My brothers and sisters, Satan knows that "*a house divided against itself cannot stand*"! When Jesus said these words, He was referring to Satan, while reflecting on Himself because the religious leaders said that He had a devil and that was how He was casting out devils, working miracles and healing people. (Mark 23:23-26)

With there being many divisions among the Church, Satan is working towards bringing us to a place of "desolation", as Jesus taught the disciples!

The Apostle Matthew recorded Jesus saying, *"Every kingdom divided against itself is brought to DESOLATION, and every city or house divided against itself will not stand"*. The word "desolation" means, the state of being decayed or destroyed, a bleak and desolate atmosphere, an event that results in total destruction.

Are you now getting the picture? Satan is trying to render us powerless in our influence in the world because we are at odds with one another and that directly goes against the real "Lord's Prayer" recorded in John 17 where He asked the Father to make us one as He and the Father are one and He said that our unity would show the world that He actually did come to the earth and redeem mankind.

If the Apostles and Prophets do not exist today then there are a great number of charlatans in the Church! Well, some of them are but not all of them!

Now for the reality check, what happens if a foundation is removed? The entire structure falls apart and crumbles (DESOLATION)!

Have you ever seen a foundation removed from an existing structure, no, you never have and you never will, it is impossible to do that so why then do you think it is so concerning the Church? The consistency of the foundation is also found within the structure because it causes the structure to remain strong and stable!

There is no such thing as a foundation not existing and the structure still being there. When a foundation is "removed", the structure has already been gone because the foundation is the last part to be removed in a demolition!

I said this to say that there are *some* Apostles and *some* Prophets just as there are still *some* Evangelists, and *some* Pastors and Teachers, so let's end this senseless debate causing our "desolation"!

Well, we are not done with this issue just yet, there is more to be said regarding this major issue of division in the Church today.

6

THE APOSTOLIC MISSION OF JESUS – PAST AND PRESENT

Jesus Christ was the only Apostle by title in the world when His earthly ministry began! He actually fulfilled all of the ministry gifts that He gave when He ascended. Jesus was the Apostle, the Prophet, the Evangelist, the Pastor and the Teacher! Jesus fully operated in all five of the ministry gifts and had 100% success in all of them!

We know that Jesus was a Prophet because He told of things to come and prophesied of many things to come. We know that He was an Evangelist because He preached the good news of the coming Kingdom of God.

We also know that Jesus was a Pastor and Teacher because He took care of the disciples and taught them what the Father taught Him.

We should know that Jesus was an Apostle by virtue of all of the prophesies and scriptures that referred to His earthly assignment before He ever came to the earth!

A true Apostle has a specific assignment or mission to complete or start. They are given the authority to carry out their mission in representation of God, Whose Name is Elohim, Himself. Their ministry has "attesting signs" following as was with the original Apostles. A true Apostle will wreak havoc on the kingdom of darkness and confront the religious systems of the world!

Jesus did all of this, but the major assignment of the Apostle Jesus Christ is that He came to redeem mankind! Jesus was *"the lamb slain before the foundation of the world"*! (Revelation 13:8)

Jesus was sent into the earth to pay the ransom for all of mankind; He was the apostle of a mission to accomplish and He executed it well!

He paid for all of the sins of mankind from the past, all sins of the present and all sins in the future! On the cross He uttered these last three words, *"It is finished"* (completed)!

Jesus Apostolic Assignment

Jesus came to ransom mankind

Jesus came to seek and save those that were lost

Jesus came to demonstrate the power and authority of the kingdom of God.

Jesus came to fulfill the Old Covenant of Law and establish the New Covenant of Grace.

Jesus came to preach liberty to the captives.

Jesus came to open blind eyes spiritually and naturally.

Jesus came to preach the gospel to the poor.

Jesus came to heal the brokenhearted.

Jesus came to set at liberty those who were oppressed.

Jesus came to preach the acceptable year of the Lord (The year of Jubilee).

Jesus also came to let the world know about the great love that Father God has for all of us and to not only cover our "sins" but remove the "penalty" of them by His "death" on the cross of Calvary, in our place!

This is the earthly mission of Jesus Christ, the "Apostle" of our faith! Guess what, His apostolic mission has not changed at all because aside from a couple of those assignments, they all still need to be maintained in the earth! This is the reason why the Apostles and the Prophets must be in existence today and operating at their fullest potency!!

Today, Jesus is still calling and anointing Apostles and Prophets to help continue His ministry in the earth just as He is calling Evangelists, Pastors and Teachers! His Apostolic mission in the earth will continue until He is crowned King of kings and Lord of lords and then turn everything back over to His Father!

7
WHY DOES THE CHURCH STILL EXISTS TODAY?

That is an easy question to answer, because many people in the world have not yet received the redemptive work of Jesus Christ! The call is still going out for those whom He foreknew to come on home and be safe from the coming judgment of the world.

Many people are sitting on the sideline waiting for a serious move of the people of God to remove the confusion in the world concerning Jesus Christ and to answer the question, exactly Who is God!!!

We, the Church, have not yet proven to the world that Jesus Christ came to the earth because we are still severely divided with disagreements on scripture and other things and separated, forming or seen as a unit apart or by itself; not joined with others!

We are not different nor are we distinct from one another, we are One, One body, One people, One nation, One holy race of people world-wide and **ONE** FAMILY, all united by the pure blood of Jesus Christ!

The Church and the nation of Israel are the only living people with testimonies of God on the earth today!! We know that according to Romans 8:19-22 that all creation groan in childbirth pains waiting for the manifestation of the sons of God, the mature ones, to be about their Father's business and do the works of Jesus so that they can be freed from the decay and bondage that has been in place since the fall of man.

We have a great responsibility to fulfill in these last day! As we come to the closing of the end of the "Church Age", we absolutely must become one in mission, generally speaking, one in judgment and of the same mind, that is, having the mind of Christ!

We are divided and separated by denominations, races, cultures, beliefs, doctrines, economics and wealth and even the lack thereof, this is to our shame! Jesus did not initiate any of these divisions and the Holy Spirit did not institute any of these division, actually, He came to bring and keep us all together, world-wide!

The late President Ronald Reagan said to the Soviet Union in 1987 "Tear Down These Walls" regarding the Berlin Wall. I am saying this to the Church, "TEAR DOWN THESE WALLS OF DIVISION THAT ARE DIVIDING THE CHURCH, THE WORLD-WIDE BODY OF JESUS CHRIST, FOR THE SAKE OF THE KINGDOM OF GOD AND JESUS CHRIST WHO IS THE KING"!!!

Right now, here in America, the government is "shut down" because of division within the Congress and the Democrats and the Republicans; this is a natural picture of the Church of Jesus Christ today, to our shame!!

The End-Time Harvest

Yes, there is an end-time harvest that the Father has been patiently waiting for and it is upon us now to begin to reap that harvest from every nation of the world for our God and Father.

Jesus said, "*the harvest is ripe but the laborers are few*"! Let's look at that passage of scripture. Ever since Jesus was on the earth, that harvest has been coming in on a daily basis but yet there are still just a few laborers!

Matthew 9:37-38 says, "*The harvest is indeed plentiful, but the laborers are few. So pray to the Lord of the harvest to force out and thrust laborers into His harvest*". (AMP) The parable of the Wheat and the Tares is an example of what is to come.

In Matthew thirteen (13), Jesus spoke of many parables but we are going to look at the one that emphasizes the harvest. Jesus said, "*The kingdom of heaven is like a man who sowed good seed in his field: but while men slept, his enemy came and sowed tares among the wheat and went his way. But when the grain had sprouted and produced a crop, then the tares also appeared*".

It goes on to say, "*So the servants of the owner came and said to him' sir, did you not sow good seed in your field? How then does it have tares?' He said to them, 'an enemy has done this.' The servants said to him, 'Do you want us then to go and gather them up?' But he said, 'No, lest while you gather up the tares you also uproot the wheat with them.*"

Jesus then said these words, "*Let both grow together <u>until the harvest</u>. I will say to the reapers, First gather together the tares and bind them in bundles to burn them, but gather the wheat into my barn.*" Matthew 13:24-30 (NKJV)

This parable speaks to the coming end of the age or world, the days that we are living in. Jesus explains the meaning of this parable starting in verse 36; He goes on to say, "*He who sows the good seed is the Son of Man. The <u>field</u> is the <u>world</u>, the <u>good seeds</u> are the <u>sons of the kingdom</u>, but the <u>tares</u> are the <u>sons of the wicked one</u>. The <u>enemy who sowed them is the devil</u>, the <u>harvest</u> is **<u>the end of this age</u>**, and the <u>reapers</u> are the <u>angels</u>*". Matthew 13:36-39 (NKJV)

Finally, Mathew continues to record this verbal transaction. Jesus then said, "*The Son of Man will send out His angels, and they will gather out of His kingdom all things that offend, and those who practice lawlessness, and will cast them into the furnace of fire. There will be wailing and gnashing of teeth. Then the righteous will shine forth as the sun in the kingdom of their Father. He who have ears to hear, let him hear!*" Matthew 13:40-43 (NKJV)

This parable speaks of the harvest being the end of this age and Jesus said, "the harvest is indeed plentiful, but the laborers are few."

He then says to the disciples to pray to the Lord of the Harvest to *force out and thrust laborers into His harvest*, the harvest being the world! It is essential that we, the laborers, be fully equipped to go out into the world (harvest) and make disciples of nations starting with the person right next to us!

The Great Commission which was given to the Apostles and the disciples by Jesus, just before He ascended back into heaven, has not changed!

We must continue this commission to the end and we desperately need the Apostles and Prophets, Evangelists, Pastors and Teachers to continue to prepare us and repair us in order to truly begin to do the works that Jesus did while He continued to teach the disciples.

Jesus said, "*Go into all the world and preach the gospel to every creature and make disciples of all nations, and he who believes and is baptized will be saved, but he who does not believe will be condemned, baptizing them in the name of the Father and of the Son and of the Holy Spirit, teaching them to observe all things that I have commanded you; and lo, I am with you always, even to the end of the age. And these signs will follow those who believe: In My name they will cast out demons; they will speak with new tongues; they will take up serpents; and if they drink anything deadly, it will by no means hurt them; they will lay hands on the sick and they will recover.*" (Matthew 28:19-20, Mark 16:15-18) NKJV

As you read that, you will notice that it is a combination of Matthew and Mark's testimony put together to see the whole transaction at that time. I took my liberty to combine the two but not to misquote what either one of them recorded according to what Jesus was saying.

This commission still require Apostles and Prophets to fulfill that mission! If you diligently search the scriptures, you will find no passages telling us that there are no more Prophets and no more Apostles. Those ministries have not yet come to an end.

The Perfecting of the Saints

Ephesians 4:12 is where this concept comes from. The "perfecting" of the saints is an ongoing task given to the designated leaders in the "Church", the Body of Christ!

In the King James Version of the Bible, the word "perfecting" of the saints is used. "Perfecting" means the *"complete furnishing, to complete thoroughly, to adjust, to frame, to mend, to make perfectly joined together, prepare and restore"*. (Strong's Concordance)

Other translations use the word "equipping" or "equip". The word "equip" means to *"supply with the items needed for a purpose or to prepare someone for a situation, activity, or* task". The word "equipping" and the word "perfecting" are interchangeable and are relevant to this specific passage.

The Apostle Paul wrote about what Jesus did when He left the earth, and that is because the Lord revealed all those things to him. Paul never walked with Jesus while He was on the earth but he did while Jesus was in His exalted position at the right hand of God. He was given many revelations!

Paul's letter to the Ephesians says, "*And He Himself gave some to be apostles, some prophets, some evangelists, and some pastors and teachers, for the equipping of the saints, for the work of ministry, for the edifying of the body of Christ*". (Ephesians 4:11-12) NKJV

These five Ascension gifts have all been given for the same general purpose or mission. It goes on to say, "*Until we all come to the unity of the faith and of the knowledge of the Son of God, to a perfect man, to the measure of the stature of the fulness of Christ; that we should no longer be children, tossed to and fro, and carried about with every wind of doctrine, by the trickery of men, in the cunning craftiness of deceitful plotting, but, speaking the truth in love, may grow up in all things into Him who is the head – Christ – from whom the whole body, joined and knit together by what every joint supplies, according to the effective working by which every part does its share, causes growth of the body for the edifying of itself in love.*" NKJV

If you look closely, there are seven (7) things that will occur when all of these ministries are working together as one, yet separately! The number Seven (7) represents Completion and Perfection in the Bible; the words "equipping and perfecting" are synonymous with the number seven!

44

This is what we achieve when all five of these ministries are active and properly functioning in the Church. To eliminate the Apostles and the Prophets from the ministries of the Church is to take the backbone and the eyes out of a person, who at that time, will be dead! Maybe that is why the Body of Christ has been generally ineffective in the world today! Division and Strife and Unbelief is still keeping us, the Body of Christ on the operating table waiting to be revived, restored and refreshed!

Please show me two or three witnesses in the scriptures that prove that Jesus stopped giving those two ministry gifts to the "Church". We have Pastors coming up like popcorn and Teachers coming out of the wood works, the poor Evangelists are stuffed in the pews without any recognition! Why do you want to terminate or exterminate the Apostles and Prophets you Pastors and Teachers?

Selah, Pause and Calmly Think About That!

8
MY FINAL ANALYSIS

The Lord gave me the assignment to write this book on Sunday, August 11, 2013 at 6:20 AM and I set it up to be written once I completed "*Fire From Heaven: And They Were All Filled*", the doctrine of the Baptism in the Holy Spirit.

I actually began writing this book on Friday, September 20, 2013 at 6:20 AM. Before I went to bed after midnight, I said to the Lord, "Is there anything else that you want to say to me for me to do"; I had just completed the manuscript "*Fire From Heaven*" on Wednesday September 11, 2013. I wrote a few things as I looked over my notes for this book and then fell asleep. That morning I was awakened by a heavy thunderstorm with bright flashes of lightning!

I arose and could not get back to sleep and the Lord began to give me more notes regarding this book so I felt the creativity and inspiration building inside of me so I knew that it was time to begin writing. I heard in my spirit, "Order in the Church" and I knew that that was another chapter that the Lord was giving me.

I believe the back to back heavy thundering and bright flashes of lightning bolts was God, Whose Name is Elohim, saying, "Order in the Church", "Order in the Church"!!!!

I sat down at the computer and He began to give me the Chapter subjects and titles, and so this book was written!

The day has finally come to bring an end to the debate regarding Apostles and Prophets! If we still have Pastors and Teachers and Evangelists, then we absolutely still have Apostles and Prophets!

It is the strategy of our adversary, the devil, to cause people to believe that they are no longer with us. He does that in an effort to divide us from each other and to bring us to desolation (come to nothing).

We know that his strategy will never come to pass, however, it does bring limitations to our "kingdom impact" against the kingdom of darkness and our influence in the world!

I believe that when the five ministry gifts that Jesus gave all come together, It will be as one big "balled-up fist" that continually pound on the enemy! Our unity is powerful with Elohim, nothing is impossible to us and we will soon experience that power and influence!

There is absolutely no scriptures inspired by the Holy Spirit that says that there are no more Apostles and Prophets today!

There are those who allowed their minds to develop this disbelief concerning that and they had help from the adversary through "theologians" who improperly applied some scriptures and then inserted carnal reasoning to support their disbelief.

Understand this, Jesus had already chosen His original twelve Apostles just as He began His ministry, approximately three years before His ascension back into heaven.

One of the twelve was a traitor leaving only eleven. The Apostle Paul came about well after Jesus was resurrected and had ascended back into heaven and he became the twelfth Apostle taking the place of Judas Iscariot. (*So when did Jesus stop raising up Apostles now?*)

Immediately after Jesus ascended, He gave the ministry gifts to men, Paul, whose name was Saul at that time, was persecuting the church and was not an Apostle, he was a murderer. Jesus began to give some to be Apostles and some to be Prophets at that time, the Apostle Paul was somewhere down the line; there were others called to be Apostles before him!

I am not here to fight against theologians or those who have this disbelief. I am here to bring us into unity, gathering ourselves around the correct application of scripture which is "the Truth" and the Truth is actually Jesus Christ, Himself!

Jesus said, I am the Way, **the Truth** and the Life, no man comes to the Father but by Me! It is high time that <u>we</u> <u>gather</u> <u>around</u> <u>Him</u>, <u>the</u> <u>Holy</u> <u>Spirit</u> and apply His wisdom to everything that we say, do and believe. We are still in a war and this is one of the warfare strategies that we must apply!   SELAH

www.ingramcontent.com/pod-product-compliance
Lightning Source LLC
Chambersburg PA
CBHW060053050426
42448CB00011B/2443